MW00639414

HOW TO RECEIVE AND MINISTER

the Baptism of the

HOLY SPIRIT

JOAN HUNTER

CHARLES AND FRANCES HUNTER

How to Receive and Minister the Baptism of the Holy Spirit
By Joan Hunter, Charles and Frances Hunter

Special thanks to Kelley Murrell for his time and God given talent that he has put into the compilation and final editing of this book.

ISBN: 978-0-9829516-1-3

Published by Hunter Books
PO Box 411
Pinehurst, TX 77362 U.S.A.

Cover design by Yvonne Parks of www.pearcreative.ca
Interior design by David Sluka

Printed in the United States of America

*D*O YOU HAVE A DESIRE FOR MORE OF GOD? Do you want to experience more of God's power than you ever have in your life? Pray about receiving the baptism of the Holy Spirit, because this is when the power of God hit our family.

John Osteen once said, "If you have a problem with speaking in tongues, don't blame me, blame Jesus! He was the first one to talk about it!"

Jesus said these words:

"And these signs will follow those who believe: In My name they will cast out demons; they will speak with new tongues." – Mark 16:17

Neither Pentecostals nor the Charismatic Movement invented speaking in tongues…God did! When my parents received this wonderful gift from the Holy Spirit and spoke in tongues, it was so glorious and so powerful that they blazed a trail across the nation and eventually the whole world just because they wanted everyone to experience what they had received from Jesus!

For three people who were totally against speaking in tongues, it was quite surprising that we developed a desire in our hearts for more of the power of God. But because we hungered for the baptism of the Holy Spirit, we were ready in our spirits and our hearts to receive from God. However, we didn't understand what the baptism was and our lack of knowledge caused us to be afraid.

We wanted to receive this endowment of power that Jesus promised. God puts the desire into each believer, but we have to be ready to submit to His will and commands before that desire can become a reality.

God used an audio message on the baptism of the Holy Spirit by George Otis to teach us how to receive His work in our lives. He gave very simple instructions of some things anyone can do. When we did them, Jesus immediately baptized us with the Holy Spirit and we fluently spoke in tongues.

The following pages contain the testimony of my mother and father, and also my own testimony of receiving the baptism of the Holy Spirit. The last chapter shows how you can receive and minister the baptism of the Holy Spirit.

Jesus said that if *we* know how to give good gifts to our children, then "how much more will your heavenly Father give the Holy Spirit to those who ask Him!" (Luke 11:13). As you read, receive the baptism for yourself and learn how to help others receive this wonderful Gift.

Chapter 1

The Testimony of
Frances Hunter

IN JANUARY OF 1971 Charles and I were in Hawaii and the Lord granted us a harvest of souls for His kingdom and new Christian friends. Some Hawaiian friends gave me two books called *Crisis America* and *You Shall Receive* by George Otis. I read *Crisis America*, which I thought was excellent, and almost threw away the other one as I had done with all other books of that nature, but didn't.

Somehow God's Holy Spirit impressed me to keep the book, so I stuck it in my luggage and thought maybe I'd read it "sometime" after I got home...but I didn't! I hid it! I didn't want anyone to find that kind of literature in my house.

In the summer of 1971 Charles and I went to the International Christian Booksellers Convention in Denver. We were at the booth where *My Love Affair With Charles* was being featured, just looking over the convention hall floor prior to our autographing session. As we looked around the huge convention room, we saw directly across the aisle from us a sign, which said, "George Otis autographing here from two to four p.m."

Then I saw a very distinguished man sitting there autographing books and I thought, "I wonder who that is." Then another thought came to my mind and I said to Charles, "Who is George Otis?" A little bell had begun to ring in my mind concerning that name and I was trying to recall what it was.

Then it dawned on me! I said, "Charles, that's George Otis!" I grabbed Charles and ran over to meet him. I remembered that this man had been a tremendous influence in the life of Pat and Shirley Boone. He was mentioned in one of their books. We had heard a lot about him in Hawaii. Then I remembered that he was the man who had written *You Shall Receive* (which I hadn't read) and others. The Lord must have wanted us across that aisle because we felt strongly compelled to meet George Otis.

We introduced ourselves, and I said, "You don't know who we are, but that's all right, because we know who you are." George Otis shocked me by saying, "Are you really Frances Hunter? I just got back from Hawaii and everywhere I went all I heard about was the way you turned that island upside down for Christ."

I was flabbergasted that anyone like him would have heard of me. I couldn't believe my ears, but I could believe the love of God that radiated from him. We talked and talked and our spirits blended beautifully with his as we shared what the Lord had been doing in our lives. There was never a moment of awkwardness as we talked, but in Christ there never is. Later that afternoon, Pat and Shirley Boone came over and we had a marvelous time praying with them as we knelt on the floor of the Convention Hall in Denver.

Then God had us do an unusual thing. We invited George Otis again to stay at our house when he was in the Houston, Texas, area. The only other people we had ever extended such an invitation to were Pat and Shirley Boone. We are out of town so much we weren't able to extend such invitations very often. However, we went out of our way to invite George Otis to stay with us.

In August of 1971 I went to the hospital for eye surgery and the way the Lord guided my recovery was fabulous. Even so, there is still a certain amount of weakness after an operation. The day after I came home from the hospital I got a telephone call from California. It was George Otis' secretary who said, "George asked me to call you and tell you he'd love to accept your invitation to stay at your house. He'll be arriving quite early that Saturday morning, so he will stay in a motel that night. You can pick him up at the Full Gospel Businessmen's meeting and he'll go home with you then. He will stay with you Saturday night if it is convenient for you."

We hadn't even invited George for that weekend, but I didn't think too much about it because we had given him a vague invitation at the Christian Booksellers Convention. I didn't realize the tremendousness of God's miracle until months later. Friends of George's had seen in the newspaper that he was coming into Houston and had called California asking him to stay with them, but God's Holy Spirit crossed the communication lines and the returning call was placed to us instead. So we received the "wrong" invitation. Wow! Praise God!

I immediately started to tell her that while we would sincerely love to have him, I had just gotten home from the hospital and it would be impossible for me to have a guest at this time. However, those words didn't come out of my mouth at all! What I did say shocked me because I said, "We'd love to have him to be our guest. We'll pick him up Saturday at the meeting."

I listened to the final instructions and then hung up the telephone and almost collapsed. The whole thing was ridiculous, but I knew it had to be of the Lord anyway. There was no way I would be physically ready to have a guest in just one more day. So, I WENT TO BED! Before I did, however, I prayed and said, "Lord, you'll have to give me the strength I need because otherwise I'll never be able to do it."

Then I picked up the phone by the side of my bed and called Charles and said, "Honey, do you know what I just did?" And then I told him. Charles is so protective where I'm concerned that I knew he'd call George's office right back and tell them I wasn't able to have company. BUT HE DIDN'T. He said in his real sweet way, "Honey, I'm sure the Lord will give you all the strength you'll need while George is here."

I fell back in bed exhausted! Then I remembered I hadn't read George's book and I thought it would be awful if I hadn't read my guest's book. I scrambled out of bed, praying all the time, "God, where did I put that book I didn't want anyone to see in this house?" Praise the Lord, He had seen where I hid it and reminded me quickly where it was. I read the first eighteen pages and then fell asleep. The minute I awoke, I picked up the book and read the rest of it. Somehow I knew then what was going to happen.

Charles and I talked late into the night about the genuineness of the gift of tongues and held to our "amended" opinion that it was genuine. It was scriptural, but it "might not" be for us. However, both of us prayed fervently that night and said, "Lord, if this is of You, let our minds be open and receptive to whatever You have for us."

The second morning after the telephone call, we were up at the crack of dawn and left to go to the Full Gospel Businessmen's meeting to pick up George. We felt obligated to go because we didn't

$\mathscr{W}$e prayed, "Lord, if this is of You,
let our minds be open and receptive
to whatever You have for us."

feel it would be polite not to attend the meeting where George was speaking. George later said he never dreamed we would attend the meeting, but there we were!

Later George said it really made him self-conscious when he knew we were present during the service in which he was speaking. He was afraid it might destroy our friendship since he thought we were against the baptism of the Holy Spirit. What he didn't know was how well the Holy Spirit had prepared us for the meeting God Himself arranged. We have often remembered this when we have hesitated in speaking to others about the baptism. Sometimes we forget that God has already gone ahead of us.

We were fascinated with George's testimony that day, seeing how God had worked in his life. The power and authority in his life were evident and his love for the Lord blazed! The Jesus in Charles and me loved the Jesus in George!

After the meeting, George held a session for those who were seeking the baptism of the Holy

Spirit. Charles and I didn't want to go. I wonder if it was because we thought someone might see and recognize us? We wanted to be close enough to hear what was being said, but not close enough to be involved. Several people approached us afterwards, so try as we might, we couldn't hear anything George said. We kept "stretching" our ears trying to hear what was going on, but couldn't hear a word. I whispered to Charles, "See, the Lord just doesn't want us to get involved with this kind of stuff!"

We had lunch with George and his Houston friends. One friend asked me, "How come George is staying with you when we asked him to stay with us?" I thought nothing of this until later when George realized God had purposely confused the telephone calls.

George came home with us and we talked about nothing but Jesus the entire time. George was speaking again that night at the University of Houston. We went too and sat right in the front, anticipating where he would put the people who came seeking the baptism. We wanted to be close enough to hear this time! We were eager to find out what was going on!

God had other plans! We were thrilled again to hear George's message, and when this meeting was over, we knew we would be in a good position to hear what was going on in the second meeting without getting involved. Two or three times during George's teaching session on the Holy Spirit we tried to slip forward, but each time we got held up by someone else. We came home and all we talked about was Jesus, Jesus, Jesus! George had never yet even mentioned the baptism. He was just bubbling over with what God was doing in those days! As we got into bed, we whispered to each other, "See, God doesn't want us involved because did you notice how He blocked us again from hearing what George said?"

But the Holy Spirit was still working, so we said, "But if You want to give it to us, just give it to us!" We lay there with our arms folded. NOTHING HAPPENED!

$\mathcal{W}$e said, "If You want to give it to us, just give it to us!" We lay there with our arms folded. NOTHING HAPPENED!

We got up the next morning to take George to a church where he was speaking. Our breakfast conversation was fabulous! Notice how God did the job as He always does and covered us with His love. God knew our greatest dislike was people who had tried to cram "tongues" down our throat, but here we were with this fabulous guest in our home and he hadn't yet said one word to us about the baptism. All we were talking about was the current miracles of Jesus.

I couldn't stand it anymore. Here we had this man in our house, one who had written books about the ministry of the Holy Spirit, and he hadn't said a single word to us about it! I said: "George, you KNOW we don't speak in tongues, don't you?" (I'm sure I must have sounded real smug!) George said one of the funniest things I ever heard because he answered: "No, I hadn't noticed!" He then went right on eating his breakfast! He didn't continue the conversation.

So I said, "We believe there is a genuine gift of tongues. There was a time we told God we didn't want it, but we realized how wrong this was, so we've told God if He wants to give it to us, we'll just take it. But we're not going to go out of our way to get it because we just don't think we need it."

Here emerged the old self-righteous Frances because I added, "The Bible says 'ye shall receive power,' and you can look at our lives and see that God has already given us power." In love George said to me, "I know the power you've got in your life because I've seen the evidence of what happened while you were in Hawaii. But wouldn't you like to have MORE power from God?"

I honestly felt like I'd been kicked right in the stomach! Who was I to tell God I had so much power I didn't need any more? I felt a little sick. I shot up a silent prayer to God apologizing for thinking that I didn't need any more power than He had already given me. Then George made a challenging statement, "Frances, you've already got ONE Hot Line to Heaven. Wouldn't you like to have TWO?" (He was referring to one in English and one in the spirit—the natural and the supernatural!)

Again that sickening feeling in the pit of my stomach! Why shouldn't I want a second Hot Line to Heaven? Why shouldn't I want a "double-portion?" Then I began to use the usual clichés I had hear so many times. "Well, then, just let Him give it to me." George came back with, "God doesn't work that way. He won't force the baptism on you any more than He will force salvation on anyone. YOU have to take the first step, then God will do the rest."

Then Charles said, "Maybe God is building a reputation for us as we share across the nation to show you can be filled with the Holy Spirit without speaking in tongues." George looked up from his breakfast and again in great love said, "Jesus worked without reputation," and another fetter broke that bound "self-righteous" Charles. (That's what Charles called himself.)

By this time, breakfast was almost over and we had to race to get dressed for the service where George was to speak. As we were walking to get into the car, I panicked because I realized that George wouldn't be back to our house before returning to California. We were to take him right to the airport after church and we still didn't understand this "tongues" business. I hadn't forgotten the two kicks that George had given me, so as we stood at the door, the words just tumbled out of my mouth: "You don't by any chance have a cassette tape or something we could listen to, do you?" George said, "I just happen to have one in my suitcase, and I'll consider it a privilege to leave it with you."

George had one unedited tape which he had felt impressed to finish just before he came to Houston—the first and only teaching he had ever made (at that time) on the baptism of the Holy Spirit. I believe God's Holy Spirit had George record it just for us! George gave us a tape called "How To Receive The Gift Of The Holy Spirit" that was to dramatically change our lives and complete the work God had been doing for years around us.

I couldn't wait to get home from the airport. I was completely exhausted by this time, so I fell into bed and suggested we play the tape. Charles, in his beautiful wisdom, knew I'd never be able to listen because I was so tired. He said he thought we'd better wait until the next night when I wasn't quite so exhausted.

I could hardly wait until Charles got home on Monday night! I had reread everything I could find on the subject of tongues all day Monday. I had searched the Scriptures, asking God to reveal the truth to me as to what He wanted in this area of my life. And all of a sudden certain portions of the Bible took on a new and greater meaning. I read and reread the book of Acts that day. When I read Acts 10:44-46...

> While Peter was still speaking these words, the Holy Spirit fell upon all those who heard the word. And those of the circumcision who believed were astonished, as many as came with Peter, because the gift of the Holy Spirit had been poured out on the Gentiles also. For they heard them speak with tongues and magnify God.

God! When did you put that new verse in the Bible? A thought came into my mind: *How could they know the Gentiles were filled with the Holy Spirit?* The last sentence really hit me, "for they heard them speaking in tongues and praising God." Was this the sign, then? Was this an automatic overflow? Was this for ALL believers? I continued reading and came to Acts 11:15:

> And as I began to speak, the Holy Spirit fell upon them, as upon us at the beginning.

In other words: "Well, I began telling them the Good News, but just as I was getting started with my sermon, the Holy Spirit fell on them. *Just As He Fell On Us At The Beginning.*"

How did Paul know the Holy Spirit fell on them? Did they immediately begin to manifest the fruit of the Spirit? How could they do so in such a short time? They couldn't because that is not possible. So I began to wonder if, when the Bible says, "the Holy Spirit fell on them, [just] as He fell on us at the beginning," it meant there was the evidence of speaking in tongues! I went back to Acts 2:4:

> And they were all filled with the Holy Spirit and began to speak with other tongues, as the Spirit gave them utterance.

Was this a manifestation of the endowment with power from on high? Then I read 1 Corinthians 14:4,

> He who speaks in a [unknown] tongue edifies himself, but he who prophesies edifies the church.

I had always misunderstood the word "edifies" and took it to mean "glorifies" himself (and I didn't think that was good), but I took time out to look it up in the dictionary and it said, "build up one's faith." And I thought, "So what's wrong with building up your own faith? NOTHING!"

I read 1 Corinthians 14:19, which I had heard so many times:

> Yet in the church I would rather speak five words with my understanding, that I may teach others also, than ten thousand words in a [unknown] tongue.

I had always heard people say about this verse: "Paul said it was ridiculous to waste your time speaking in tongues because five words in your own language are better than ten thousand in an unknown language." They were right, but Paul was referring to speaking IN THE CHURCH. He didn't say anything in that verse about the privacy of your own prayer closet. I had always heard that verse used as one of the strongest arguments against speaking in tongues, but all of a sudden it began to speak to me in a totally different way.

I realized for the first time that there were two kinds of tongues! One gift is for public use, which is one of the nine gifts of the Holy Spirit and the other is for your private prayer life. I realized the Bible wasn't teaching that speaking in tongues was wrong, but that there was a place and time for that expression. I backed up and read some more.

The Bible wasn't teaching that speaking in tongues was wrong, but that there was a place and time for that expression.

I started at 1 Corinthians 12 and read it over and over. I got out the New English Bible, the Living Bible, the American Standard, the Revised Standard, the King James Version, and every translation that I had. They all said about the same thing!

I quote from the New English Bible:

> There are varieties of gifts, but the same spirit. There are varieties of service, but the same Lord. There are many forms of work, but all of them, in all men, are the work of the same God in each of us, the Spirit is manifested in one particular way, for some useful purpose.

Listen to the Living Bible:

> Now God gives us many kinds of service to God, but it is the same Lord as we are serving. There are many ways in which God works in our lives, but it is the same God who does the work in and through all of us who are His.

Suddenly I "grew up" enough to understand that God had never said that we were all going to have the same gifts, abilities, or callings. God never promised to treat each one of us exactly alike. God had never said He wanted all of us to serve Him in exactly the same manner. He did say there were all kinds of gifts, and all kinds of services, but it is still the same God who does the different kinds of work in and through all of us who are His.

◆ 29 ◆

I read every translation in our house and they all included the same message. When they got to verse 28 and listed the gifts of the Spirit, every version includes the gift of speaking in tongues. Some refer to it as "ecstatic utterances," or "languages they have never learned." There isn't a single translation of the Bible that leaves out this gift. Every translation includes the gift of tongues along with all the other gifts. Why, then, do we act like God made a mistake when He included this gift right along with the eight others? The Bible seals the fact that it IS a gift of the same Holy Spirit who gives all other gifts. Wouldn't we have to deny all of them as relevant for today if we deny one?

Well, how about the fact that it is listed last? When Paul said, "Earnestly desire the best gifts" (verse 31), doesn't this mean we should desire those listed first? Does Paul indicate anywhere which is the most important of the gifts? Frankly, I would like even the least of one of God's gifts, wouldn't you?

He does say, however, that even if you speak with the tongues of men (your own mother tongue) and of angels (your heavenly language) but have not love, you are nothing! It doesn't say the gift is nothing. It says you are nothing if you exercise the gifts of the Spirit without love. I again remembered all the arguments I had heard about the gift of tongues being listed last and that being the reason we shouldn't seek that one. Paul said seek ALL of them, and at one time or another, we read of each of them working in Paul's life.

My thinking was changing—rapidly! I thought of the years when I had said, "God, I DON'T want that gift. That's no good!" Then I remembered that for years I had said, "Well, God, if You want to give it to me, that's OK." Then I thought about what HE was saying to me today. He was saying, "You've sought all the others, why not this one?"

With that, the last of my defenses folded, but I was still confused because I didn't realize that what I was seeking was the gift of the Holy Spirit, not the "gift" of tongues.

We bolted our supper down that Monday night and quickly finished anything else we needed to do in the house. Then we hurried to bed, turned on the tape and listened. Before we listened, we prayed fervently, asking God to do whatever He wanted to do with our lives. We prayed, "God, if this is a new dimension You want in our lives, then we are willing to take the first step and boldly ask for it."

Neither of us said a word until the end of the tape because we had been listening so intently. We had heard teaching from the Word that really made sense. We realized that in accepting the gift of salvation, each of us must take the first step and that

$\mathscr{W}$e prayed, "God, if this is a new dimension You want in our lives, then we are willing to take the first step and boldly ask for it."

God then does the rest. We had to cry out to God for forgiveness of our sins and ask Jesus to come into our hearts before either of us experienced it. We realized, "It's the same with the baptism of the Holy Spirit; we have to take the first step."

We were especially impressed with one point. Remember when Peter walked on the water? Peter himself had to put his foot over the side of the boat, and only then did Jesus make the water hard—hard enough for him to walk on. When Peter not only trusted Jesus' word to "Come!" but acted on it, the miracle happened.

We listened intently as the tape gave the instructions—nearly all of it Scripture—and yet mentioning the fact that as intelligent adults we might feel somewhat foolish. But God puts a premium on obedience and approaching him as a little child. George Otis emphasized the need to pray for Jesus to baptize with the Holy Spirit and then for each person to begin to speak as the Spirit gives the utterance.

George had suggested that we raise our hands in worship and surrender to God. There we lay, side by side, hands raised in worship to God. When the tape said, "Now," the silence in our room was deafening. You couldn't even hear us breathing. NOT A SINGLE SOLITARY SOUND CAME OUT OF EITHER ONE OF US! I couldn't have uttered a sound for anything!

I looked at Charles and said, "Honey, why didn't you say something?" Charles looked back at me and with his fabulous dry sense of humor he said, "Honey, George said to not think, just to let sounds come out and I can't make a sound without thinking. So I didn't do a thing!"

We decided we needed to listen to part of the tape again, so we did, and when we came to the part when George said, "Now," we both raised our hands above our heads, looked at each other, and began laughing like a couple of idiots. I don't believe I had ever felt so ridiculous in my entire life. I didn't know that I could be self-conscious around my beloved husband, but I was. We decided the Lord didn't want us to try this together, so we turned off the tape recorder and went to sleep.

I couldn't wait for Charles to go to work the next morning! Usually I kiss him three thousand times before he goes to work and I'm still hanging onto him because I hate to let him go, but this particular morning I was practically shoving him out the door.

The minute I heard his car go around the house, I ran for the bedroom. I didn't even take the breakfast dishes off the table. The Holy Spirit was really quickening my heart and I jumped back into bed and turned on the tape recorder. The thing that really stood out in my mind was how Jesus had made it possible for Peter to walk on the water.

Alone now, I listened to the whole tape again up to the part where George said Now! Then I turned off the tape recorder. There was no one in the room but Jesus and me, but the power and presence of God was as real as it had ever been in my life. I softly whispered a very simple little prayer, "God, if this is genuine and real and really of You and it's for me, then do a miracle for me as you did for Peter when he walked on the water. Jesus, I ask You to baptize me with the Holy Spirit."

In that moment of yielding to God of my mind, my soul, my spirit, my tongue, my brain, I gave just one or two little sounds, and instantly I was baptized with the Holy Spirit. The room was filled with the most beautiful glow you could ever imagine. I had to close my eyes! The splendor of the Lord was there! The entire room seemed bathed with the love of God. I thought surely I must be in heaven. Never have I felt such a helplessness before God as I did in that moment of yielding. Gone were the barriers I had built up ever since I became a Christian about the matter of praying in tongues. Out of my own mouth flowed the most beautiful "love" language in the world. I knew I was praising and loving God just like the disciples on the day of Pentecost.

I have never felt closer to God, more loved by God, more protected by Him, more sheltered by Him, or overflowing in love and praise for Him than in those moments. My cup was running over!

I couldn't understand a word I was saying, but I knew God could. My heart knew that in my overflowing love for the One who had so changed my life, I was the praising His Holy Name, and I wasn't cluttering up the praise with some of my own inadequate words, but was using the special "love" language that He had given to me. Jesus speaking of this had said, "From [your] innermost being will flow rivers of living water" (John 7:38, NASB).

I could have kept praying in tongues all day; it was so glorious! But the Lord reminded me of my husband, so I quickly called Charles. All I said was, "Honey, it's true! There is a beautiful heavenly language and I've got it!" Then I began to cry. Praise the Lord and pass the Kleenex. Then Charles began to cry too. Praise God for his tender heart! He said, "Let me hear you."

At that time I believed I had to have my hands over my head to speak in tongues. Since I was holding the telephone, I told him it was impossible. Charles said, "Please try, Honey!" So I "scooched" down in bed again, trying to hold the decorator

*I*n my overflowing love for the
One who had so changed my life,
I was the praising His Holy Name.
I wasn't cluttering up the praise with
some of my own inadequate words,
but was using the special "love"
language that He had given to me.

phone on my shoulder and still keep my hands up in the air!

I hadn't forgotten! Over the telephone I prayed in the Spirit for Charles. All he could say was, "It's beautiful, Honey, it's beautiful." As the power of God melted the telephone wire with love, I told Charles the one thing that had helped me was asking Jesus to do a miracle for me as He had for Peter.

Then I prayed, "Lord, so that we will stay on the same spiritual level, I ask that You baptize Charles with the Holy Spirit and give him a heavenly language in the car on the way home tonight."

It was a blessed day! I prayed in English! I prayed in tongues! I praised God in English! I praised God in tongues! I sang in English! I sang in the Spirit!

The glory of the Lord never left our house that day! I had gone to the store when Charles came home and for once he was glad I wasn't there. (He wanted to pray alone.) When Joan and I later drove in the driveway, Charles raced out to meet us and I knew by the expression on his face what had happened. God had answered our prayer! He didn't even wait for me to ask the question because he knew I was going to ask, "Did you receive your special language?" He simply said, "I did!"

Then it was my turn to cry! I had asked God to bless Charles the same day and He did! What rejoicing! What wild joy! What love of God!

(Not everyone has the same emotional reaction that we had at the moment of receiving the Holy Spirit. Remember it isn't a matter of feeling, but obedience that counts.)

God had woven the final gossamer thread, but it didn't turn out to be a web at all. It turned out to be a lovely bow on another of His beautiful gifts just for us. This was a REAL gift accompanied by a special "prayer" language to be used for Him and for His purposes.

Chapter 2

The Testimony of

Charles Hunter

YIELDING MYSELF to what God wants has been one of the most exciting experiences of my life. Jesus yielded His desires so completely to those of His Father that the two were one. Probably the biggest reason I couldn't relate to this was that I was trying to serve Him on a part-time basis. He made His commands very clear to the Israelites, but they wanted other things more than pleasing God. It was the law and not love that motivated them.

As a carnal Christian I used to try to obey the law, which really was more the law of my own church. My church told me speaking in tongues was a "no-no" and the doctrines of man molded my attitudes. The Holy Spirit was now absorbing my every thought and desire, but I was suspicious and doubtful about this gift so clearly offered in the New Testament. I was hesitant to venture away from the safe harbor of my teachings—my church law.

For a time I was attending another church that did not even teach the simplicity of salvation: asking God to forgive our sins and Jesus to come into our lives and control our desires and thoughts. One Sunday the minister, whom I love very much, began his sermon by saying, "I don't care what 'they' say; I'm going to preach this sermon." He then preached a beautiful message with the plan of salvation in which Jesus gave His life for sinners.

For one day this pastor risked the security of being controlled by the rules of his denomination, which were the same barriers that stood between me and the baptism of the Holy Spirit. These are the same walls within which denominations so often theologically enslave their people and keep them from the freedom God wants them to experience.

My unwillingness to relinquish man-taught doctrines in favor of seeking the instructions of the Holy Spirit in concert with the Bible was a wall that stood between me and the gift of the Holy Spirit. We will not understand the truths in the Bible if we refuse to seek His will. We only understand God's promises after we, by faith, obey what He says. We must take the first step.

Frances and I share all our thoughts with each other and because our minds are constantly focused on God and Christ Jesus, we are constantly seeking to know His will. We were doing this one day as we flew from the Pacific Northwest to Los Angeles. We were talking about God and about whether tongues should be a part of our lives. We doubted

$\mathcal{M}$y unwillingness to relinquish
man-taught doctrines in favor of
seeking the instructions of the
Holy Spirit in concert with the Bible
was a wall that stood between me
and the gift of the Holy Spirit.

they would be and in this way we also cast doubt on God's Word. Our usual reply to questions about the baptism of the Holy Spirit was that we were willing to receive this gift, but that God apparently had other plans for us.

Then we read the book *A New Song* by Pat Boone. We were made aware of the beauty and genuineness of this gift. It was not referred to by this disturbing word *TONGUES*, but was described as the *heavenly language of love* as Shirley, Pat, and their daughters each were given their own individual praise language to be spoken just during their private times with God. Somehow, I knew there was more to what happened to them than just a "thing" called "speaking in tongues." My heart melted in a pool of love as I read their testimony.

Since Frances told you about our encounter with George Otis and his visit in our home, I will just mention some of the other advances the Holy Spirit made through him in my life. We were well aware that George spoke in tongues and believed that his visit with us was planned and timed perfectly by God. We were eagerly anticipating his arrival. When we heard George's testimony and felt the power of the Holy Spirit in him, our confidence in his relationship to God was complete. The love, joy, peace, gentleness, and other fruit of the Spirit radiated from him.

George became a vessel of God's love in our lives as the Holy Spirit used him to prepare our hearts and minds for His work. In the informality of our breakfast room even as we discussed the subject of tongues, I believe the Holy Spirit had already won the doctrinal battle over tongues and had given us a wholehearted desire for this gift.

Two days later my heart leaped with excitement as Frances shared with me the beautiful new language God had bestowed upon her only minutes before. Tears of joy filled my eyes as this beautiful language flowed from her lips. I didn't understand the words, but my spirit understood their significance. God was so thoughtful and considerate! That whole day I was working at the side of at least one other person, but for the few moments Frances was on the phone with me, everyone had left the room. God gave me some privacy to feel the new depth of His love in Frances and the fresh fragrance of the Holy Spirit as she shared her new language with me.

After Frances called that morning, I could hardly keep from bubbling over with excitement. I had almost uncontrollable eagerness to get through my work day so that I would be free to go home and accept the gift I was certain God had for me. I was working in downtown Houston that day and as soon as the work day ended, I rushed to my car and moved into the heavy rush hour traffic. I had been praising God all day (I have learned to "think of God" as I work) and now I was asking Him to prepare my spirit to receive the gift of the Holy Spirit as soon as I reached the freeway.

I get excited whenever I have a special gift for Frances or Joan. I can hardly wait to give it to them. God loves to bless us also with abundant gifts and I'm sure He was as excited as I. He seemed to move cars out of my way so I could rush onto the freeway. Just as soon as I rounded the curve which leads onto the freeway, I prayed, "Jesus, I ask you to baptize me with the Holy Spirit and give me a heavenly language just as you did Frances."

If you think Frances had a problem raising her hands trying to balance the telephone on her shoulder while lying down, you should have seen me! I was driving sixty miles an hour in heavy freeway traffic. (You don't really have to raise your hands to be baptized in the Holy Spirit. However, it is necessary to raise your heart in love and praise to God, to keep your spiritual eyes on Jesus lest you sink back into self as Peter did.)

I simply opened my mouth and a beautiful, new, wonderful heavenly language of love poured out of me! The car was flooded with the glory of God as I yielded my deepest desires to Him in a new found release. What magnificent and overwhelming joy I experienced as I felt the very presence of Jesus as the Holy Spirit within me was speaking with my mouth, my voice, my tongue—directly to my Father in heaven. Jesus said He had made provision

$\mathcal{I}$ felt the very presence of Jesus as the Holy Spirit within me was speaking with my mouth, my voice, my tongue—directly to my Father in heaven.

for us to go into the very presence of God Himself. At that moment I felt completely under the power of the Holy Spirit and that I had released myself to His control. This mighty miracle of streams of living water flowed out of my mouth as the Holy Spirit gave utterance without the direction of my human mind. Hallelujah! The "heavenly language" continued to flood my soul all the way home for the next twenty minutes.

For the only time in my married life, I prayed that Frances and Joan would not be home so that I could submerge myself into God's presence alone. I rushed into our study and looked to the heavens as the joy of the Lord came upon me while I praised Him all alone in my beautiful new language of love for thirty wonderful minutes. Then I heard her car come into the driveway and ran with outstretched arms to my sweetheart. In bursting joy I simply said, "I did!"

How we thanked Jesus for baptizing us with the Holy Spirit and bestowing upon us our heavenly language of praise!

Chapter 3

The Testimony of

Joan Hunter

MY PARENTS WANTED ME TO RECEIVE the baptism of the Holy Spirit very badly. They had people lay hands on me everywhere we traveled and usually IN FRONT OF A CROWD. Talk about putting me on the spot! It caused me to clam up, then shut up! I had an interesting time watching them after they had received the baptism. I saw miracles and the release of God's power like I had never even heard about.

I want to tell you of some of the things that happened to my parents during this time. They would go to a church service, come home, and tell me ALL about it. They demonstrated what they saw by dancing and praising God with tambourines and other kinds of worship items, then singing in the spirit. They would get the pans out of the kitchen and bang them with wooden spoons like tambourines and sing. Their voices were not the best! Then I asked myself, "Do I really want this?"

I can laugh about it now, but then I was WAY concerned for them because it appeared to me that they had lost their minds. I tried and tried to speak in tongues.

About this time I went off to Oral Roberts University. The first year there I did NOT have the baptism. I came home from school for the summer and was so frustrated. I wanted it so bad. I went into the room where I was sleeping. I lay down and I said to God, "If this is of you, I want it. I want

ALL you have for me." Just as I finished that prayer the language started to flow. It flowed and flowed and flowed. It was May 16, 1973. I was so excited the date got branded in my mind.

I prayed for hours. It was such a special time for me and the Lord. No one laid hands on me and no one STARED at me. It was just God and me alone together. From that moment on, I felt His presence like never before. I could communicate in His language and pray according to His will, not mine. This day changed my life forever. I received the power that I had longed to receive from Him—to see the blind see, the lame walk, the hurting healed, and so much more.

I went to the Philippines with my mom and dad around 1977 and at the time I was a quiet timid person. When Mom and Dad ministered the baptism, they always wanted me to pray with those who were receiving. One night while I was praying in the spirit with those receiving, a man came up to me to let me know I had given the plan of salvation in perfect Hebrew. It was overwhelming to me to hear that. There will be times when unusual things like this happen. God may choose to use this gift in unique ways. However, most of the time tongues cannot be understood by the human mind.

In Mark 16:17, Jesus commanded us all to speak in tongues, so that is what we wanted everyone to do. Jesus also said,

> "Go therefore...teaching them to observe all things that I have commanded you." – Matthew 28:19, 20

The Great Commission is a command, not a suggestion, for us to GO AND DO! That also means that we need to be able to teach and equip the saints to minister the baptism of the Holy Spirit.

We studied everything we could about how the baptism was ministered in the New Testament. Jesus ministered directly to people without laying hands on them. Paul ministered by the laying on of hands. We have done both and it works either way. We have ministered to forty or fifty thousand people at one time. There is no way we could lay hands on that many people, but they received the same Holy Spirit anyway because Jesus is the Baptizer.

We discovered that when we instructed people in simple language the way we were, that hungry Christians would receive the Holy Spirit and speak in tongues just as we had. The Bible tells us:

> "Out of his heart will flow rivers of living water." But this He spoke concerning the Spirit, whom those believing in Him would receive; for the Holy Spirit was not yet given, because Jesus was not yet glorified. – John 7:38-39

We discovered that when we removed the mystique and misunderstanding that had entered into the minds of many about what God wants to do for us as believers, that it would simplify their receiving from the Holy Spirit. Jesus worked in the supernatural in a very natural, non-religious way. As we share how to receive and minister the Holy Spirit, we make a specific effort to help people to relax. We are simply vessels used by God to release the supernatural in the lives of others.

Our way of ministering the Holy Spirit is not the only way. If you do things differently and it works for you, continue doing what has been effective for you. However, we have seen millions of people receive the Holy Spirit. So if we can help you through this booklet, then please adopt any part or all of what you learn here and work together with us to equip the saints to do the works Jesus commanded.

You are the one to whom we are ministering now, so visualize yourself either receiving the ministry of the Holy Spirit or ministering to someone else as you read the next chapter.

Chapter 4

Receiving and Ministering the

Baptism of the Holy Spirit

YOU ARE ABOUT TO RECEIVE what the Bible calls the baptism of the Holy Spirit, or the gift of the Holy Spirit. Your spirit is about to be filled completely with God's spirit, and just like Jesus instructed, you will speak in a spiritual language as the Holy Spirit gives the utterance. As I take you through these steps for yourself, they are also exactly what you would do with others who want to receive the baptism of the Holy Spirit.

You must be born again before receiving the gift of the Holy Spirit. So to be sure you are born again, pray this prayer with me:

> Father, I have sinned. I ask You to separate my sins from me and put them on the cross of Jesus Christ. I ask You, Jesus, to come into my heart and live Your life through me. Thank You, Jesus, for coming into my heart and for making me the kind of person You want me to be. Amen!

When you are born again, your spirit is filled with the Spirit of Jesus. Romans 8:9 says,

> But you are not in the flesh but in the Spirit, if indeed the Spirit of God dwells in you. Now if anyone does not have the Spirit of Christ, he is not His.

Charles saw his spirit outside of his body in 1968 and it looked identical to his physical body. Even his face was the same. The only difference was that he could see through his spirit form as if it were a thin fog or cloud.

All languages are made up of many different sounds. We must make the sounds, but the Holy Spirit will give the utterance as we speak. Speaking in tongues is supernatural. It's a miracle! It's a sign and a wonder which Jesus Himself said would follow those that believe.

We are asking Jesus to baptize us with the Holy Spirit just as sincerely as we asked Him to save us from our sins. He will do His part if we do ours. The people who received the Holy Spirit on the Day of Pentecost were ordinary human beings just like us, yet they spoke in tongues they did not know.

Paul said,

> I will pray with the spirit, and I will also pray with the understanding.
> – 1 Corinthians 14:15

$\mathcal{W}$e are asking Jesus to baptize us with the Holy Spirit just as sincerely as we asked Him to save us from our sins. He will do His part if we do ours.

When you pray with your spirit, you do not think about the sounds or the language.

In a moment when I tell you to, begin loving and praising God by speaking many different syllables, but not in a language you know. Don't try to reason your way through this process. When you speak in tongues, you are verbalizing out of your spirit and not from your mind. In the beginning it is best to make the sounds rapidly so you won't try to think as you do in speaking your natural language.

Continue making the sounds with long flowing sentences. Don't make a few sounds and stop and start. Let them flow like rivers of living water. Make the sounds loudly at first so you can easily hear what you are saying.

Most of all, love and praise God. You are speaking directly to God in His perfect will when you pray in tongues, or in the spirit 1 Corinthians 14:2 says:

> For he who speaks in a tongue does not speak to men but to God, for no one understands him; however, in the spirit he speaks mysteries.

Romans 8:27 says:

> Now He who searches the hearts knows what the mind of the Spirit is, because He makes intercession for the saints according to the will of God.

Each time I minister to someone or a group, I speak in tongues, talking to God in my spirit language so people can hear what my language sounds like as an example or demonstration of speaking in tongues. I speak naturally and at a normal volume, but expressively. This does not need an interpretation because I am talking to God. When God talks to an assembly of people through a message in tongues, that must be interpreted. 1 Corinthians 14:27-28 says:

> If anyone speaks in a tongue, let there be two or at the most three, each in

> turn, and let one interpret. But if there is no interpreter, let him keep silent in church, and let him speak to himself and to God.

To help people understand that this is a supernatural language, I often tell a story about one time when the Spirit impressed me to speak in tongues. I looked right into the eyes of a young woman standing among about 150 people to whom I was ministering. Very expressively I spoke in tongues to her and they all received the Holy Spirit and spoke in tongues. Later this young woman came running to me and told me the following:

> I am a Jew. For years I couldn't believe that Jesus was the Messiah, but I have been born again now and I know He is my Messiah. When you told us to make those funny little sounds and God would give us a spirit language and empower us with His Holy Spirit, all kinds of doubts came into my mind.

I thought I couldn't receive and that it wouldn't work for me. I was about to give up and leave when you looked straight at me and in a perfect Hebrew (and I don't know a word in Hebrew!) you said, "Relax and it will come easily." When you said that, I knew it was God. I opened my mouth and the language was there.

You will not understand the language you are speaking because it is an unknown tongue given to you by the Holy Spirit. If you do not have a fluent language, let me illustrate why you don't. Say this phrase with your understanding loudly (when you are ministering to others, have them do this as well):

Jesus, I love You with all of my heart!

OK, now, say this out loud:

Jesus, I…

Why did you stop making sounds? Did you notice that when you stopped making the sounds, you stopped speaking? The reason some don't speak fluently in tongues is that they tried to think of the sounds and they cannot flow with the spirit analytically. So when we pray this prayer and you start speaking in your heavenly language, don't try to analyze what you are about to say, just make the sounds!

Now, are you ready to receive? Pray this prayer with your understanding:

> Lord Jesus, I thank You for the most exciting gift of all—the gift of salvation. Jesus, You promised another gift, the gift of the Holy Spirit. So I ask You, Father, to baptize me with the Holy Spirit right now, exactly as you did your disciples on the Day of Pentecost. Thank You, Jesus! You have done Your part and now I am going to do my part.

Then say:

65

66

I am going to lift my hands up to God (you lift your hands and also have others lift their hands when you minister to them); I am going to look up to God (I do this so they won't try to be religious and look down with their eyes closed, taking their attention off of God), and when I say, "NOW," I am going to begin to praise God and I want you to join me, but not in any language we know because we can't speak two languages at one time.

Father, I love You; I praise You; I worship You; I love You with all of my heart.

Ready? ONE, TWO, THREE. NOW! (You immediately begin to pray loudly in tongues and SO DO THEY!)

Let them pray for quite some time in tongues. Then stop them suddenly and say,

The devil doesn't like what you just did. He knows you have just received the power of God with which you bind him and protect you from his kingdom of demonic spirits, sickness, and lies he wants you to experience. He said to Jesus when he tempted Him, "*If* you are the Son of God…" He tried to put doubt in the mind of Jesus and he will try to put doubt into your mind."

The devil puts little thoughts into your mind like: "That didn't sound like tongues would sound or even a language to me. I could tell it was me speaking (and it IS you). I could tell it was because I could tell I was thinking and Charles told me not to think!"

Then the devil will probably tell you, "You don't feel any different…You don't feel any power." Jesus didn't say you would *feel* power. He simply said you would *receive* power when the Holy Spirit came upon you, and you have! (Acts 1:8)

*J*esus didn't say you would *feel* power. He simply said you would *receive* power when the Holy Spirit came upon you, and you have!

The way to get rid of the doubts is to speak in tongues. He can't stand tongues because he can't understand tongues. Tongues is your hot line to heaven (1 Corinthians 14:2).

This time, pray twice as loudly, twice as fast, twice as long, and with more expression of love to God and the devil will flee and take your doubts with him.

ONE, TWO, THREE. NOW!

I let them pray for a few minutes in tongues and then stop them abruptly. Once you have received the gift of the Holy Spirit, you can pray in tongues anytime you want.

Then I share:

> Now, let's pray again in our new heavenly language, but this time, let's pray with a purpose. Jesus said, "But you shall receive power when the Holy Spirit comes upon you; and you shall be witnesses to Me." This time, I want you to picture in your mind someone you

know who doesn't know Jesus as their Savior. This time you will be a witness for Jesus as you pray softly, meaningfully, and naturally in tongues, but just above a whisper.

I start praying in tongues very softly and they all do the same. This helps people realize that speaking in tongues is natural, even more natural than speaking in their known language, because they don't have to think in order to pray in the spirit.

Right after the apostle Paul said, "I will pray with the spirit, and I will also pray with the understanding," he said:

> I will sing with the spirit, and I will also sing with the understanding.
> – 1 Corinthians 14:15

So right now, you yourself lift your hands up high toward God, keep your eyes open and SMILE as you sing praises to God in the supernatural.

When I minister to someone else or a group of people, I begin singing in tongues and they begin to sing in harmony with one another in a most beautiful supernatural song).

Now, it is time for your final instructions: Pray in tongues many times a day. Paul said,

> I thank my God I speak with tongues
> more than you all.
> – 1 Corinthians 14:18

Sing in tongues many times a day too. I suggest that you sing in tongues when you are driving on the freeway, but please don't close your eyes!

Read your Bible as much as you can because now the Spirit of God in you is the Spirit of truth, and He will unveil the hidden meaning in the Bible to you now more than ever before. I suggest that each time you start to read the Bible, you pray, "Father, please reveal in Your Word what I can do for You...not just what You can do for me," and God will change your life.

Among other things, you now have the spiritual resources to minister healing, cast out devils, and do all the works of Jesus. Learn to use that power and ask God to bring someone to you every day to whom you can minister. He will, if you will!

We expect God to bring people into our pathway for ministry, and He keeps us busy. Recently in a paint store, we met a concrete finishing contractor and asked him to come to our office to bid on a job.

While we were talking with him, I discovered he was hungry for the baptism of the Holy Spirit. I ministered to him and in just a few moments he was fluently speaking in tongues. He needed healing in his back and neck, so we ministered to him by "growing out his legs and arms." He was totally healed. He watched this in amazement and said, "I've always wanted to see a miracle and I just did!"

It turned his life around instantly and he could not stop talking about Jesus. He was witnessing to the men who came to help do the work. He witnessed to the people where he bought concrete. He also witnessed to his wife who had received the baptism long ago.

$\mathcal{L}$ earn to use the power of the
Holy Spirit and ask God to bring
someone to you every day to whom
you can minister. He will, if you will!

He had attended a Spirit-filled church for four years. Why did he have to wait so long to receive what God wanted him to have all along? Most people do not know how to minister the baptism of the Holy Spirit. It is easy to do this kind of ministry when you follow these simple instructions, and especially when the Spirit of God has made people hungry for more of Himself.

Read these instructions several times and then as soon as possible minister the baptism to someone God sends to you. You will be so excited when they receive that you will never stop until Jesus comes back again!

GO AND MAKE DISCIPLES! Hallelujah!

Tools & Resources

"For the equipping of the saints for the work of the ministry" (Ephesians 4:12).

Joan Hunter and her parents, Charles and Frances Hunter, have prepared the most effective, the most powerful and simple teaching resources in the world to train ordinary believers to do the works Jesus told us to do. In just a few short hours, ordinary Spirit-filled Christians can learn to minister healing, salvation, deliverance, and the baptism of the Holy Spirit effectively. Jesus said to make disciples, and these tools will accomplish exactly that for your church, missions, or evangelism ministry.

Pastors and Churches: You can hold your own video healing school under your leadership, and train your people to go into homes, shops, streets, and wherever your people are, winning others to Jesus with signs and wonders following them daily. Consider what this will do for your church!

Evangelists and Teachers: Around the world, whether in crowds of a few or tens of thousands, you can expand your regular meetings into Healing Explosions by having healing teams trained before you arrive.

Do your normal evangelism or teaching, and then turn the trained healing teams loose to minister individually. Then have your teams do follow-up work and see the lasting results of your ministry!

Missionaries: Why try to do it all yourself? Hold video healing schools among the nationals (or home missions) and train them to be witnesses like Peter, John, and James! Jesus told us to win the lost, and "GO! MAKE DISCIPLES." Expand your results and do it like Jesus!

For more information write or call:

Hunter Ministries

PO Box 411

Pinehurst, TX 77362

Email: info@joanhunter.org

www.joanhunter.org | www.happyhunters.org

Books by Charles & Frances Hunter

The Two Sides Of A Coin

Excellent for anyone who has not yet received the baptism of the Holy Spirit. The Hunters, from an evangelical background, had been taught that "tongues" was of the devil. Read how they found the truth.

How To Heal The Sick

A true classic! Jesus said that those who believe will lay hands on the sick AND they will recover. This is the book that teaches the simple ways this commandment can be fulfilled in the life of every believer.

Handbook For Healing

Companion book to *How To Heal The Sick*. Indispensable reference guide with alphabetized listing of diseases and the most effective ways of ministering healing to those affected by them. Four new chapters!

How To Receive And Maintain A Healing

Why do some get healed and others don't? Why do some get healed only to lose the healing later? Knowing how to keep your healing is just as important as knowing how to get it!

www.joanhunter.org | www.happyhunters.org

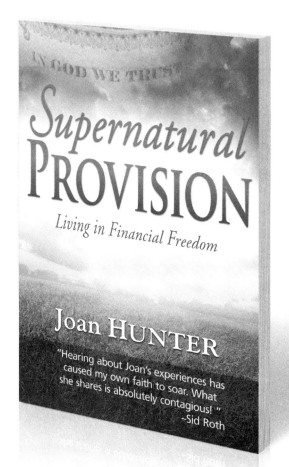

G OD'S PROVISION IS A RIVER that flows in-
dependently of our economies and abilities. He is calling
us to a place of obedient dependency so that we can receive all we need
directly from Him. Our source has no limits and our trust is in Him, not
our governmental leaders.

Joan's book puts the focus back on the eternal covenant between
God and man, highlighting His provision for His children. She shows
how you can get into His river of blessing and stay in that place. This
book will give you all the information you need to enter into God's
supernatural provision for your life.

CDs & DVDs by Joan Hunter

Can I Truly Forgive? – CD/DVD

Joan shares this life-changing teaching on forgiveness from her own personal experience of betrayal. A perfect message for those who are struggling to forgive and want to move into the freedom of a clean, whole heart.

Erase the Pain of Your Past – CD/DVD

Have you ever called out to God to change your past? Do you carry pain and remorse in your heart over the things that you have done and said? Or things that were done or said TO you? This teaching is for those who want to see God erase the pain of their past and restore all that has been lost.

Renewing Relationships – CD/DVD

Ever tried to fix your spouse or your children? Joan tells you how to do it God's way and renew intimacy in these important, God-given relationships.

For more information:

Hunter Ministries

PO Box 411

Pinehurst, TX 77362

Email: info@joanhunter.org

www.joanhunter.org | www.happyhunters.org